DISCARD

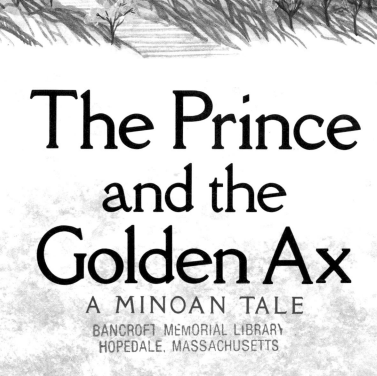

The Prince and the Golden Ax

A MINOAN TALE

Deborah Nourse Lattimore

HARPER & ROW, PUBLISHERS

To
Linda Zuckerman

The Prince and the Golden Ax
Copyright © 1988 by Deborah Nourse Lattimore
Printed
in Singapore. For information, address
Harper & Row Junior Books, 10 East 53rd Street,
New York, N.Y. 10022. Published simultaneously in
Canada by Fitzhenry & Whiteside Limited, Toronto.
1 2 3 4 5 6 7 8 9 10
First Edition

Library of Congress Cataloging-in-Publication Data
Lattimore, Deborah Nourse.
    The prince and the golden ax.

    Summary: A proud Minoan prince challenges the
Goddess Diktynna, who first offers him rewards for
his courage but then threatens to destroy Thera, his
homeland, when his boasting angers her.
    1. Diktynna (Greek deity)—Juvenile literature.
[1. Diktynna (Greek deity)   2. Mythology, Greek]
I. Title.
BL820.D54L38 1988   292'.13   87-21193
ISBN 0-06-023715-5
ISBN 0-06-023716-3 (lib. bdg.)

Storyteller's Note

Once, in ages now long past, an ancient people called the Minoans ruled the Aegean Sea. The beauty of their time filled the isles of Crete and Thera long before the arrival of the Greeks and all the gods of Olympus. Yet one day they vanished. Among the ruins were found a statue of a goddess and a double-bladed ax. Who is she, and what mystery lies behind her shining weapon? No one knows. But those who dream of such things tell this tale. . . .

4

One summer morn the skies blushed a rosy hue across the island of Thera. The great fleet drew up its sails and set off for the island of Crete and its royal city of Knossos, home of the Goddess Diktynna.

Princess Illyra sat under the ship's canopy. She touched the powerful charms about her neck and smiled at her younger brother, Akros.

"Remember, Akros," she said. "You are a great hunter and I have the gift of spells, but the Goddess Diktynna is greater still. We will be wise to honor her powers above our own."

"I will remember," said Akros. "But once the people of Knossos see my skills at the Feast Day Games, they will know who the greatest hunter is! Thera has been without glory or a champion for too long. Isn't our homeland, with its sparkling waters, tall black cliffs, and wild blue monkeys the fairest island in all the seas?"

Soon the royal ships swept into the harbor of Crete. Tanned sailors pulled up oars, and the royal procession stepped onto the rock-bound coast. Diktynna's Priestess greeted them.

"Come see the statue of our Goddess, Diktynna, and her Golden Ax, the source of all her powers," the Priestess said.

8

Akros and Illyra stared into a wooden shrine. Small axes made of bronze and silver were set into its doors and walls. Diktynna's ivory face shone in the sunlight, and her raven tresses tumbled about her shoulders. Then Akros saw the great golden hunting ax that hung from the statue's neck. He knew that it could bring glory to Thera. A hot desire rose in his heart to possess it.

9

Diktynna's Feast Day Games began with foot runners and boxers. Dancers swirled garlands before her shrine. Akros strode through them all, leading a monumental, prancing bull.

He freed the bull, then turned and leaped over its horns like a swallow in flight.
Higher and higher he jumped, until his legs swung around the bull's thick neck; then
Akros brought it fighting to the ground. The crowd cheered.

"I am a great hunter!" announced Akros to the crowd. "Perhaps I am greater than Diktynna herself! Yet *I* have no golden ax!"

At that moment the ground shook. A loud and terrible groaning sound tore through the earth. Illyra fell to her knees and pulled her brother down beside her.

13

Later, inside the palace, the Priestess spoke.

"You have challenged the Goddess," she said. "Diktynna will not tolerate such boasting, even from one so young!"

"Forgive him," said Illyra. "My brother was foolish. What offering can we make to your Goddess to cool her anger?"

"Prince Akros," said the Priestess, turning her stony gaze toward him. "Capture, if you can, the golden-scaled fish of the Eastern Isle. If you succeed, you will win a bronze ax. But if you fail, the Golden Ax will cut a path so deep through Thera, your homeland, that all its people shall perish and its ashes will be scattered far and wide."

Akros did not stop to think.

"I will do it," said Akros.

Honey-fingered dawn drew up the sky as Akros and Illyra made ready to sail. Diktynna's shrine was gently lifted onto a platform near the ship's cabin. Then fifty oars of the finest cedar struck the waves.

"We must watch for any spell the Goddess sends to stop you," said Illyra.
"Let her send a spell," said Akros. "I will still catch the golden-scaled fish."

Illyra pointed down where a faint glimmer of gold shone below the waves. Akros plunged into the rolling water. Sea spray circled where he sank. Twice he dove, each time stroking with all his might, but the spinning water whirled him away.

Illyra took a small charm from her neck.

"Little golden charm," she whispered. "Capture the circle of the sea!"

Illyra cast it far beyond the wake of the ship. It rolled away briskly, drawing the whirlpool with it, and sank from view.

Unhampered by the currents, Akros's strong arms scooped up the shining fish and flung them onto the deck. The Priestess laid them before the shrine.

"This task was too easy," said Akros.

"Akros!" gasped Illyra. "Did you forget the Goddess's spell?"

"What is a spell to a strong youth from Thera?" asked Akros boldly.

The ship heaved upward and the shrine itself began to shake.

"More boasting!" said the Priestess. "Since you are such a strong youth, see if you can capture the griffin of the Western Isle. Succeed and win a silver ax. Fail, and you shall lose your homeland. And be careful, or the power of our Goddess will turn against you."

So it was that on the second dawn, Akros and Illyra sailed to the Western Isle and the enchanted garden of the griffin.

"It will not be easy to capture the griffin," said Illyra. "His beak and talons are sharper than a bronze dagger. You can't seize him as you did the bull."

"I will outsmart the griffin," said Akros. "Soon Thera, our island, will have the Goddess's Golden Ax and the greatest glory in all the seas."

Illyra and Akros stood beside a pool whose water had long since dried up.

"This can be a trap," she said. "I will weave a leafy cover for it."

"We can gather these fruits for bait," said Akros, reaching up. "The griffin will see it and come to eat. Then he will fall into the trap."

But each fruit withered at his touch.

"Another spell," said Akros angrily. "Diktynna wants me to fail!"

Suddenly, a wild, birdlike cry pierced the air. The branches shuddered and out flew the griffin.

25

"Little golden charm," whispered Illyra, taking another from her neck. "Chase the spell from this garden!"

She threw the charm into the trees. As soon as it touched the branches, the fruit ripened again and fell into the trap. The griffin lunged forward after the fruit and fell in headlong. Akros hurled the leafy cover over him.

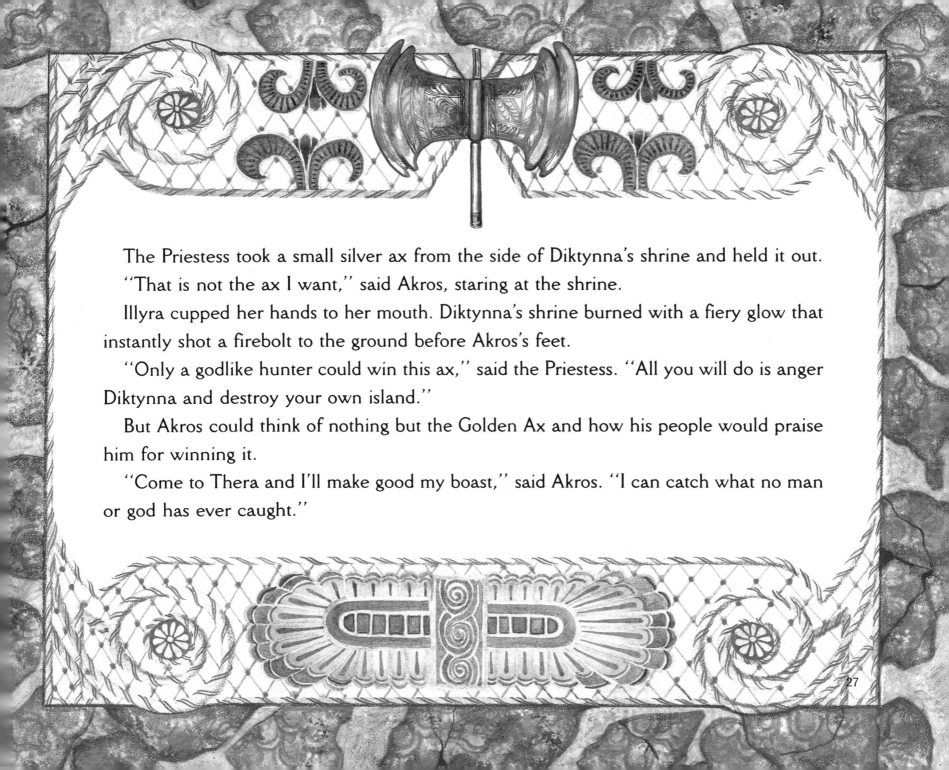

The Priestess took a small silver ax from the side of Diktynna's shrine and held it out.

"That is not the ax I want," said Akros, staring at the shrine.

Illyra cupped her hands to her mouth. Diktynna's shrine burned with a fiery glow that instantly shot a firebolt to the ground before Akros's feet.

"Only a godlike hunter could win this ax," said the Priestess. "All you will do is anger Diktynna and destroy your own island."

But Akros could think of nothing but the Golden Ax and how his people would praise him for winning it.

"Come to Thera and I'll make good my boast," said Akros. "I can catch what no man or god has ever caught."

Akros and Illyra struck out for their homeland. When their ships glided into the harbor of Thera, Illyra felt a chill in her heart. She worried over what deed Akros planned. On all of Thera, only the sacred blue monkeys had never been caught by man or the gods.

By midday Akros, Illyra, and the Priestess were high on the steep cliffs, with the shrine of Diktynna carried behind them. As they turned up the jagged path, the small temple of the blue monkeys came into view.

"Now I see what you mean to do," Illyra said. "But this time I won't help you. The blue monkeys are sacred, and it is forbidden to touch them."

Akros did not listen to his sister. He raced and leaped over the rocks, chasing after the blue monkeys. But they were too lively and quick for Akros and darted away from him, chattering and screeching.

"Illyra!" shouted Akros. "Help me!"

Illyra did nothing. She watched Akros run from rock to rock until he had chased every monkey into the temple.

Akros and Illyra looked in. Where seconds before the monkeys had climbed and swung, there was a terrible silence. Only their painted images on the walls of the temple remained. No one could catch them now.

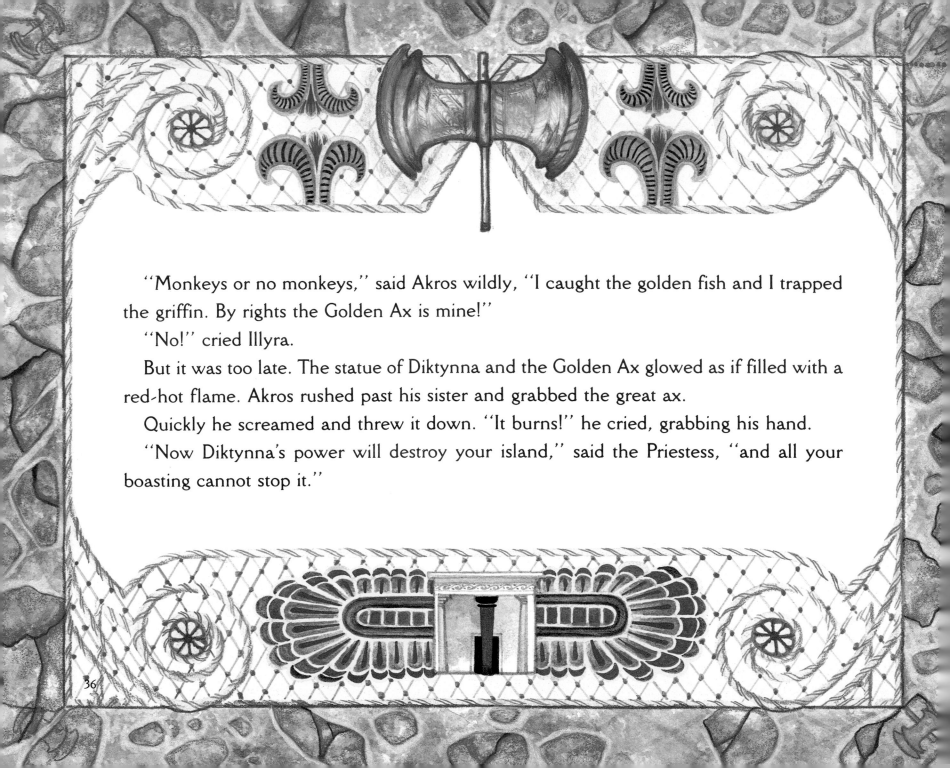

"Monkeys or no monkeys," said Akros wildly, "I caught the golden fish and I trapped the griffin. By rights the Golden Ax is mine!"

"No!" cried Illyra.

But it was too late. The statue of Diktynna and the Golden Ax glowed as if filled with a red-hot flame. Akros rushed past his sister and grabbed the great ax.

Quickly he screamed and threw it down. "It burns!" he cried, grabbing his hand.

"Now Diktynna's power will destroy your island," said the Priestess, "and all your boasting cannot stop it."

"Come," Illyra said to Akros, pulling him toward the path. "Perhaps we can still escape."

By the time Illyra and Akros were safe on their ship, the Golden Ax had already begun to cut a path through the very soul of the island of Thera. A stream of fire spilled from the temple on the mountain peak and raced to the shore.

With a last shudder, the island raised the shoulder of the sea and sank beneath the waves. The great cities, the tall black cliffs, the ancient and beautiful people were gone forever. The ships washed out into the cool Aegean, toward the faraway coast of Greece.

For many days the ashes of Thera rained down on Crete and the other islands of the Aegean Sea. And after many centuries, when the palace of Knossos was dug from its ashen tomb, a small clay statue of a goddess was found. Beside it was a small clay ax. Who put them there none but the ancients know. But we do know that such small offerings were sometimes given to gods and goddesses as gifts for times good and bad. Perhaps a young prince, wiser through the test of fire, sailed from distant Greece and placed them there along with his heart.